GAME DAY

GET READY FOR A FOOTBALL GAME

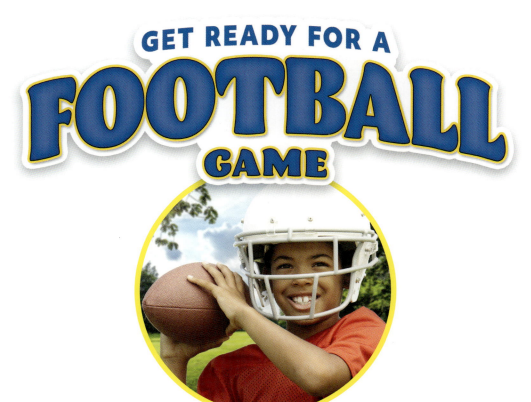

by Emma Huddleston

Consultant: Beth Gambro
Reading Specialist, Yorkville, Illinois

Minneapolis, Minnesota

Teaching Tips

Before Reading
- Look at the cover of the book. Discuss the picture and the title.
- Ask readers to brainstorm a list of what they already know about football games. What can they expect to see in this book?
- Go on a picture walk, looking through the pictures to discuss vocabulary and make predictions about the text.

During Reading
- Read for purpose. Encourage readers to think about preparing for a football game as they are reading.
- Ask readers to look for the details of the book. What needs to happen before the big game?
- If readers encounter an unknown word, ask them to look at the sounds in the word. Then, ask them to look at the rest of the page. Are there any clues to help them understand?

After Reading
- Encourage readers to pick a buddy and reread the book together.
- Ask readers to name two things from the book that a player does to get ready for a football game. Find the pages that tell about these things.
- Ask readers to write or draw something they learned about football.

Credits:
Cover and title page, © Monkey Business Images/Shutterstock and © songdech17/iStock; 3, © Gizelka/iStock; 5, © jpbcpa/iStock; 7, © Ernest Prim/Adobe Stock; 9, © jane/iStock; 10–11, © monkeybusinessimages/iStock; 13, © SDI Productions/iStock; 14L, © Moussa81/iStock; 14R, © Willard/iStock; 15, © Lucky Dragon USA/Adobe Stock; 16–17,© vndrpttn/iStock; 19, © SUSAN LEGGETT/Shutterstock; 21, © LSOphoto/iStock; 22T, © buzbuzzer/iStock; 22M,© gpflman/iStock; 22B, © skynesher/iStock; 23TL, © Veniamin Kraskov/Adobe Stock; 23TM, © NickyLloyd/iStock; 23TR, © RichVintage/iStock; 23BL, © groveb/iStock; and 23BR,© leezsnow/iStock.

Library of Congress Cataloging-in-Publication Data.

Names: Huddleston, Emma, author.
Title: Get ready for a football game / by Emma Huddleston.
Description: Minneapolis, Minnesota : Bearport Publishing Company, [2024] |
  Series: Game day | Includes bibliographical references and index.
Identifiers: LCCN 2023002705 (print) | LCCN 2023002706 (ebook) | ISBN
  9798888220566 (library binding) | ISBN 9798888222522 (paperback) | ISBN
  9798888223710 (ebook)
Subjects: LCSH: Football--Juvenile literature. | Football players--Juvenile
  literature.
Classification: LCC GV950.7 .H84 2024 (print) | LCC GV950.7 (ebook) | DDC
  796.332--dc23/eng/20230126
LC record available at https://lccn.loc.gov/2023002705
LC ebook record available at https://lccn.loc.gov/2023002706

Copyright © 2024 Bearport Publishing Company. All rights reserved. No part of this publication may be reproduced in whole or in part, stored in any retrieval system, or transmitted in any form or by any means, electronic, mechanical, photocopying, recording, or otherwise, without written permission from the publisher.

For more information, write to Bearport Publishing, 5357 Penn Avenue South, Minneapolis, MN 55419.

Contents

Football Time 4

How to Play 22

Glossary 23

Index 24

Read More 24

Learn More Online 24

About the Author 24

Football Time

My brother runs fast.

He grabs the ball.

What a catch!

It is time for some football.

Tomorrow is game day.

My brother is ready!

He has been **practicing** all week.

The **coach** showed his team what to do.

The team ran to get in good shape.

They practiced throwing and catching the ball.

The night before the game, my brother is hungry.

Our family has chicken and rice for dinner.

My brother eats an apple, too.

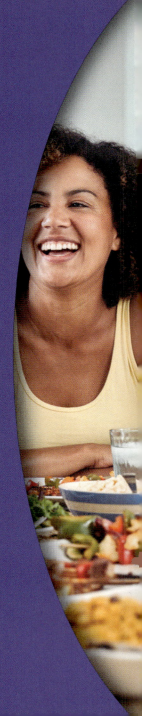

Then, my brother needs to rest.

We go to bed early.

Getting lots of sleep will give him energy.

On the day of the game, my brother gets dressed.

He ties his **cleats**.

Pads and a **helmet** keep him safe.

At the field, he **stretches** with his team.

They run up and down the field.

This gets them ready for the game.

It is time to warm up.

My brother throws the ball to his friend.

He catches the ball when it comes back.

At last, the game starts.

My brother's team is ready.

They do their best when they work together.

I love football!

How to Play

In football, two teams play against each other. They each have eleven people on the field at a time.

A game has four parts called quarters. There is a break between each.

To score points, the team tries to make it from one end of the field to the other.

22

Glossary

cleats shoes with bumps on the bottom for gripping the ground

coach the person who teaches and leads a sports team

helmet a hard hat worn to keep the head safe

practicing doing something many times to get better

stretches moves the body to pull muscles longer

Index

catch 4, 8, 18
coach 8
dinner 10
field 16, 22
practicing 6, 8
stretches 16
team 8, 16, 20, 22
throw 8, 18

Read More

Leed, Percy. *Football: A First Look (Read about Sports)*. Minneapolis: Lerner Publications, 2023.

Omoth, Tyler. *Football Fun (Sports Fun)*. North Mankato, MN: Capstone, 2021.

Learn More Online

1. Go to **www.factsurfer.com** or scan the QR code below.
2. Enter **"Football Game"** into the search box.
3. Click on the cover of this book to see a list of websites.

About the Author

Emma Huddleston lives with her family in St. Paul. She enjoys being outside while playing and watching sports!